BRITISH CASTLES
COLOURING BOOK

First published 2016
Reprinted 2017, 2023

The History Press
The Mill, Brimscombe Port
Stroud, Gloucestershire, GL5 2QG
www.thehistorypress.co.uk

Text © The History Press, 2016
Illustrations by Martin Latham, Chris West,
Tom Kilby and Sarah Austin © The History Press, 2016

British Library Cataloguing in Publication Data.
A catalogue record for this book is available from the British Library.

ISBN 978 0 7509 7024 2

Cover colouring by Lucy Hester.
Typesetting and origination by The History Press
Printed in Turkey by Imak

BRITISH CASTLES
COLOURING BOOK

The History Press

Take some time out of your busy life to relax and unwind with this
feel-good colouring book designed for everyone who loves castles!

Absorb yourself in the simple action of colouring in these majestic buildings from around
England, Scotland and Wales. From historic fortresses to romantic ruins, you are sure to
find some of your favourite locations waiting to be transformed with a splash of colour.

There are no rules – choose any page and any choice of colouring pens or pencils
you like to create your own unique, colourful and creative illustrations.

Harlech Castle, Gwynedd, North Wales ▸

Sherborne Castle, Dorset ▸

Portchester Castle, Hampshire ▸

Lowther Castle, Cumbria ▶

Windsor Castle, Berkshire ▸

Cardiff Castle, South Wales ▸

Warwick Castle, Warwickshire ▸

Skipton Castle, North Yorkshire ▸

Tattershall Castle, Lincolnshire ▸

Bamburgh Castle, Northumberland ▶

Arundel Castle, West Sussex ▸

Nottingham Castle, Nottinghamshire ▸

Berkeley Castle, Gloucestershire ▸

Powderham Castle, Devon ▸

Caernarfon Castle, Gwynedd, North Wales ▸

Sudeley Castle, Gloucestershire ▶

Norwich Castle, Norfolk ▶

Colchester Castle, Essex ▸

Pembroke Castle, Pembrokeshire,
south-west Wales ▸

Bolton Castle, Yorkshire ▸

Carew Castle, Pembrokeshire, south-west Wales ▶

Herstmonceux Castle, East Sussex ▸

Beaumaris Castle, Isle of Anglesey,
north-west coast of Wales ▸

Ludlow Castle, Shropshire ▸

Bruce Castle, London ▶

Manorbier Castle, Pembrokeshire,
south-west Wales ▶

Wray Castle, Cumbria ▶

Edinburgh Castle, Lothian, Scotland ▶

Conwy Castle, North Wales ▸

Lincoln Castle, Lincolnshire ▶

Leeds Castle, Kent ▶

Corfe Castle, Dorset ▸

THE GREYHOUND

Dunster Castle, Somerset ▶

Inverness Castle, Scottish Highlands ▶

Alnwick Castle, Northumberland ▸

Balmoral Castle, Aberdeenshire, Scotland ▸

Chillingham Castle, Northumberland ▸

Stirling Castle, Scotland ▸

Dover Castle, Kent ▸

Raglan Castle, Monmouthshire, South Wales ▸

Carisbrooke Castle, Isle of Wight ▶

Beeston Castle, Cheshire ▸

Eilean Donan Castle, Scottish Highlands ▸

Framlingham Castle, Suffolk ▸

Hever Castle, Kent ▸

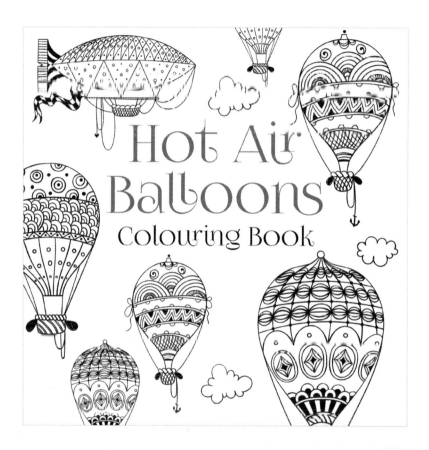